BREAKING FREE TO BE ME

Breaking Free to Be Me

Inspiring Reflections along the Highway From Breakdown to Recovery

KATRINA EVANS

Tanzanite

Tanzanite Publishing

A catalogue record for this book is available from the National Library of Australia

Interior & Cover Layout: Pickawoowoo Publishing Group
Interior artwork: Laila Savolainen, Pickawoowoo Publishing Group

ISBN(s): 9780648908203 (Paperback)
ISBN 9780648908210 (Hardback)
ISBN 9780648908227 (Ebook)

Disclaimer
This book is not intended as a substitute for the medical advice of physicians directly or indirectly for any technique as a treatment for mental or physical problems. You may consult a physician in matters relating to your health in regards to any symptoms that may require diagnosis or medical attention. The author's intention is to offer general information in support of your journey for body, mind and spiritual wellbeing. The author assumes no responsibility for your personal actions.

To all those who want to 'break free' from anxiety and depression to become a happier YOU!

LETTER TO MYSELF

Dear Myself,

I want to let you know that I can see that you are not feeling that strong at the moment with handling some deep issues you are going through. I hear you and understand this is not easy for you and hasn't been for quite some time.

It isn't fair that you have had to go through this, but I hope you realise that many other people experience these sorts of struggles and it is quite normal to feel that you are unable to cope. You are not alone and none of us are perfect. We all go through times when things are difficult and seem to get on top of us. You might even think that you have finally lost your mind.

I want you to know that you are going to be okay. You will get through this and the sun will shine again if you want it to. You just got caught in a deep rut from the dark side of life and didn't know how to get out of it, but you can now that you are hearing what I am saying and you know that I support you. I have been with you through everything in your life and will continue to be with you all the way, forever!

One thing you need to do is to start to believe in yourself and build up your confidence in that. Recognise your talents and abilities-they are there, you just need to find them and work on them.

For quite some time your mind has been closed off to hearing the good, positive side of yourself that is 'Me'. You were not able to listen to what I have always been trying to tell you, because all you could hear was the negative, bullying side that overwhelmed you and threatened to swallow you up whole!

I am so glad that at last you are now beginning to hear Me, the positive, encouraging, nurturing, and optimistic side that gives you peace, love, reassurance, security and happiness. You already have all this around you. There are plenty of people (friends, family, support groups/networks, counsellors) and reading material that can all help you to recognise this, but you need to keep practising applying the positives to yourself, while nurturing and taking care of yourself too.

You know, the bully side of you has developed over a lot of years and can be very overpowering, so you need to build up more strength and flexibility in your thinking to be able to bounce back and outsmart him.

So be patient and take one step at a time. You will get bet-

ter. I can already see you starting to grow. And remember—
I am here for you. I have got your back, always!

Love from Me. xo

NOWHERE LEFT

When there is nowhere left to run, what choices do I have but to live or die, so I must work hard at living. I have a mountain to climb, but I need not ascend it on my own.

CREATE TODAY

I will not let the past rob me of the future I can

create today.

Today can be great and tomorrow

can be greater.

HAVE FAITH

I have faith in myself,

even if I don't yet believe it,

and I have the power to get well.

The road might get rough,

but it is the highway

that I must travel to truly break free

and find the better me.

OPEN EYES

It may feel like everything

is going wrong sometimes,

but you only need to open your eyes

a little wider to see there are also

plenty of things going right.

THE LIGHT

Something beautiful can often be discovered

from every trial in life

if only we seek to notice the small ray of light

that makes it's way through

the storm clouds.

STORMS

Many of the storms that come our way

often turn out to be a lot less

threatening than our minds have

made them out to be.

GOD STRENGTHENS

Down but not out.

Lost but finding.

Despairing but never defeated.

Weak but my God strengthens me.

GROWING

A baby learns to crawl.

A child learns to walk.

An adult runs then returns to the child

to learn to walk again.

KEEP GOING

If you don't know where you are going,

keep exploring.

If you don't know what you want to be,

keep discovering.

If you don't know who you are,

keep searching- you have always been there.

BELIEVE

Never lose sight of your achievable goal,

however small it may be.

Believe in yourself.

Accept yourself as you are,

and Trust yourself with all that you do.

KEEP TRYING

Never stop trying.

If Plan A didn't work, try Plan B.

If Plan B didn't bear any fruit, try Plan C.

If Plan C produced some fruit but not enough

to last you for the season, then try Plan D.

Keep trying and eventually you will succeed.

BREATHE

Stress, Anxiety, Tension- Stop the world,

it's making me dizzy!

Slow down, Breathe, Release.

The world is now a more peaceful place.

LET GO

Fear halts and paralyses us.

Rising above fear lets us move forward.

Anxiety ties us up in knots.

Letting go of anxious thoughts frees us

from our own ropes and chains.

DREAMS

If your dreams never seem to come true,

maybe you are just looking in the

wrong direction.

TEARS

When the tears come, let them flow.

It is okay to cry.

Crying is natural and necessary.

It is the mind's way of processing emotions

and the body's way of releasing them to

make way for what comes next.

BE STILL

Stand still for a while.

Rest. Reflect. Process.

You don't need to be constantly moving forward.

And being still is much better

than going backwards!

LEARN

You will sometimes hit the odd bump in the road a bit

hard, but rather than seeing it as a deep pothole

and you have failed, try looking at what you can

learn from it.

Having the courage to continue on with the journey

in spite of these setbacks will really strengthen you

and take you a long way.

TIME PASSES

Most difficult situations will resolve

themselves over time.

What looked like today's disaster will soon become

yesterday's unfortunate event.

SIMPLE

It's okay to keep things simple.

Life can be complicated enough.

BUILDING

To successfully build a mansion,

you need to start with building a sandcastle.

THE BODY

Eat well, exercise and keep fit.

Look after your body-it has held you up and

kept you breathing all your life.

CONTROL

Learn to let go of the things you don't

need to control. Don't worry- the world will

still keep revolving just fine on its own, as it has

always done since the beginning of time.

A PROBLEM

Some things are not worth worrying about.

A problem is only a problem if it bothers you.

SMALL STEPS

Glance over your shoulder now and then and

acknowledge how far you have come.

Praise and reward yourself for the progress you

have made even if you have only taken little steps.

It is the smaller steps that will get you

further in the long run than the one big step

that became too much for you.

FORGIVENESS

You can't change the past and what happened

to you or what you did. Learn to forgive others

instead of holding on to bitterness towards them,

but most importantly- learn to forgive yourself.

PRESSURES

Wife, mother, friend- Me.

That's all I need to be.

Let go of the pressures you put on yourself.

CARE

Care less about what other's think of you.

Care more about what you think of yourself.

PATIENCE

Be patient with yourself. Recovery is a gradual

process and it takes as long as it needs to.

OLD WAYS

Don't be hard on yourself when you do slide

backwards sometimes.

Old ways of thinking and acting are difficult to shift

as they can be strangely comfortable, like a pair of

worn out slippers.

INNER CHILD

Look after your inner child.

What does he or she need to hear from you?

UNIQUENESS

Embrace the unique person that is You.

You are one of a kind and that kind has much

to contribute to the diversity of our world

and to what keeps it ever turning.

CAPABLE

You are capable of transforming into a new, improved, more content version of yourself who has grown from having gone through trial and suffering.

EXPERIENCE

What you have gained from your experiences along

your journey will equip you for the next chapter of

your life, so enjoy the ride and observe the scenery.

It's not so much about reaching your destination

-it's more about the interesting towns you have

gone through on your way there.

GOOD DAY

Today can be a good day if I so choose it to be.

It doesn't always need to depend on

my circumstances.

PACE YOURSELF

Drive at a speed that you can handle.

Don't let the tail-gaters push you to go faster,

including your own self.

A WAY

Don't let the cars that brake in front of you stop you from moving forward. There is usually a way of getting around them.

I CAN

Change your "I can't" into "I can"...

at your own pace, in your own way, and within

your own limits.

BE OPEN

Listen to the advice of trustworthy people,

especially the words of wisdom from doctors

and other health professionals.

Always be open to hearing the voice of

the most qualified expert who really knows you the

most intimately- You.

RELAX

Don't give up fighting to get well, but don't fight so

hard that you forget how to relax and let life flow.

MAKE PLANS

Structure your day with plans to include activities you enjoy doing. These are what will make you want to get out of bed in the morning and keep you motivated to face the day.

FUNNY SIDE

Life is no joke, but it ought not to be taken too seriously either. Seeing the funny side of things can really lighten your load, especially when you learn to laugh at yourself too.

GOOD ENOUGH

I am Me.

I am good enough.

I am who I am and I can be myself beyond

what I ever imagined I could be.

THE PRIZE

Life is a precious gift, so allow yourself to

receive it's prize.

You deserve to enjoy living.

ACKNOWLEDGEMENTS

Special thanks to:

'Hope Garden' by Bec Thorpe (2011) Blurb, for inspiring me to write in this style and format.

'Centre for Clinical Interventions' at the following website: www.cci.health.wa.gov.au for their resources and study modules, especially Module 5:Self-Compassionate Thinking (Building Self-Compassion- Compassionate Letter Writing) which I used to help me construct the 'Letter to Myself'.

And all the people who have shared their knowledge and/or supported and encouraged me over the years including doctors, nurses, therapists, clergymen, support workers and groups, family and friends, and especially God!

www.ingramcontent.com/pod-product-compliance
Lightning Source LLC
Chambersburg PA
CBHW070633150426
42811CB00050B/286